Performance Training
For Youth Athletes

GAGE STRENGTH TRAINING

KEY CONTRIBUTOR
Jeff Schumacher

2012 Graduate of Penn State University; Jeff earned
a bachelor's of science degree in Kinesiology. While at
|Penn State, Jeff served as a Strength and Conditioning
intern for 17 Varsity sports. Jeff returned to school to earn
a Master's Degree in Exercise Sciences (focus on Performance
enhancement and Injury Prevention) from California
University of PA in 2013. While at CalU, Jeff worked as
a Strength and Conditioning coach for the Philadelphia
Union (MLS).

TABLE OF CONTENTS

CHAPTER ONE
Introduction

Hi, I'm Jeff Schumacher.

I wrote this book for parents, coaches, and athletes of all ages and skill levels who want to improve overall sports performance. This text will cover the fundamental principles of athlete training, debunk myths, and provide training tips used by elite professional athletes. My goal with this book is to help athletes reach their highest athletic potential in a safe and effective manner.

Safety is one of the primary focuses of my work and this book. I've seen many poorly designed, risky training programs. Some set the athlete up for injury. Others do not provide a mechanism for athletes to reach their full potential. All these programs are a waste of the athlete's time. I value the time and the health of the individuals I train, and I have developed this program to enable them to achieve maximum benefit for the training time invested, while keeping safe from injury.

I've been coaching athletes for six years and have a broad base of experience that uniquely qualifies me as a trusted resource for guiding young athletes. I have an undergraduate degree in kinesiology from Penn State University, and a masters of exercise science from California University of Pennsylvania. I have coached professional athletes in every major sport (NBA, NFL, NHL, MLB, MLS), and I was on the coaching staff of the Major League Soccer team the Philadelphia Union. I was also part of the coaching staff of two Big Ten championship teams. I've trained two NBA All-Stars and several MLS All-Stars when I was with the Philadelphia Union.

I've accumulated a tremendous background of training and hands-on experience, and want to pass as much of it as I can on to others who feel as passionately about sport as I do. I hope you will benefit from my learnings as you read this book and apply the techniques within to your own training and coaching.

CHAPTER TWO
Getting Started with
Performance Training for Youth Athletes

Performance training is training with a specific goal to improve your performance in a competitive setting. Performance training can be used to enhance every aspect of athletic performance, including speed, agility, quickness, strength, power, endurance, flexibility/mobility, body composition, and injury prevention.

Safety is a concern with athletes of all ages, but especially for youth. Every parent and coach should know that youth performance training is safe, provided the athlete is working with a knowledgeable coach who creates safe and effective programs. Parents are right to be wary because many coaches and trainers lack sufficient training and knowledge, and consequently they make mistakes when training younger athletes. Common mistakes include loading young athletes with weights, such as a barbell, before they have practiced or shown efficiency in fundamental movement patterns. Another mistake coaches often make is creating programs without specific goals in mind. Yet another common error is demanding too much volume from their athletes in the form of sets/reps, sessions, or training time. Lastly, some coaches and even parents believe their athlete didn't get a good workout unless they left the session dog tired. The truth is every training session doesn't have to be a killer, and in fact, too much fatigue may set the athlete up for injury.

The program outlined in this book is designed to avoid those pitfalls, keep the athlete safe, and improved performance. My approach is a progressive program in which the athlete starts at the ground level and progresses slowly through each subsequent phase. On Day 1, the athlete is not moving weight with a barbell, rather he or she is moving only body weight. The goal is to demonstrate functional movement quality with little compensations. For some athletes, it may be months before they begin using weights at all. The key is to be smart in the fashion that you progress the athlete though each phase of training and to avoid progression overload.

Progression overload causes injuries. Injuries set the athlete back, delaying progress and possibly even causing permanent damage. While this is a risk with all training activities, it happens frequently among young athletes following poor training protocols. In the next chapter, we will examine the discipline of strength training in greater depth.

CALL 610-567-3433 TODAY FOR A FREE CONSULTATION/
TRAINING SESSION AND TAKE YOUR GAME TO THE NEXT LEVEL

CHAPTER THREE
Strength Training for Athletes

Strength training is exercise that uses resistance in order to build stronger muscles and increase the size of the skeletal muscle. Many amateurs go into the gym and hyper-focus on one or two muscle groups. Men, for example, love to develop their arms and chest. The goal when conducting strength training for an athlete is not to focus on individual body parts, but rather to address the full body as a whole. Training goals for general population may be increasing the size of the biceps or losing belly fat, whereas training goals for an athlete need to take the whole body and all its systems into consideration

This program focuses on training every facet of human movement. The days of seated leg curls and biceps curls are over. After all, when was the last time you saw an athlete sitting on their butt on the court or field? The most effective athletic strength training must be performed in a functional fashion. Sports are played in an ever-changing environment. Training in a similar fashion garners the best results.

Let's look at an example. Traditional strength training may focus on three major lifts such as the bench press, the squat, and the deadlift. Athletic strength training will also center around those; however, you have to incorporate movement correctives, mobility, power, speed, agility, quickness training, and most importantly, injury prevention work. Traditional strength training doesn't incorporate all the components of fitness. Injury prevention is critical. It's no longer about, "Oh I've got bigger biceps," or, "My calves are not big enough." It is about the body being used as a whole.

CHAPTER FOUR
Speed, Agility, and Quickness Training for Athletes

SPEED

Speed is simply the rate at which you are able to produce a movement, or how fast your body is able to complete an action. In the case of running, for example, speed is how fast the runner is completing his or her strides. The person who can stride the fastest is going to be the fastest runner.

When dealing with young athletes, speed is important because at that age, they are not going to have yet developed great technical skill in their sport. Generally, the fastest athletes are the best athletes at the youth level. It is very important, especially at a young age when they are still learning the fundamentals and the nuances of the game itself, to be able to leverage the natural speed talent of the young athlete.

Speed is the result of genetic gifts and training. For each individual, there is a maximum potential speed they will be able to achieve; however, achieving that potential is dependent on proper training. You can only reach your full potential if your training program is built properly, so while the raw material for speed is genetic, if you are not training for speed, you are not going to be able to fully develop that genetic material.

Many parents ask, "Can my kid get faster?" The answer, generally, is yes. An athlete gets faster by understanding and focusing on the science of speed training, which includes posture, strength, force production, core strength, acceleration, deceleration, and stride length and frequency.

Posture. Maintaining correct posture while running is extremely important. When starting a sprint, the body ideally needs to be at a 45-degree angle. An upright runner faces a little more wind resistance and will be slower than a runner that has a good forward lean.

Limb posture, also referred to as limb mechanics, is equally critical for speed generation. The body needs to move efficiently, so the way the limbs are moving is extremely important. Poor limb mechanics equals a poor runner. On the other hand, strong limb mechanics equals a strong runner. Ideally, elbows should be at 90 degrees coming from behind the hip to the cheek on each stride, and the runner should have a high, straight knee drive on each stride. Arms should not cross the midline of the body.

Strength and force production. For forward movement, strength and force production are interdependent factors. In order to move faster, you need to create more force. Greater force production equals greater ground reaction force sent back to you. The more energy you create, the more energy the ground will return to your muscles, and being stronger will allow you to put more force into the ground when making a stride. This in turn generates greater speed.

Core strength. Core strength goes hand in hand with posture. A stronger core improves your overall posture, and posture will give you control at top speed.

Acceleration and deceleration. Acceleration is the ability to reach maximum speed as fast as possible. Deceleration is the ability to control the body when stopping or slowing down.

Stride length and frequency. Stride length and frequency are the keys to speed. The athlete with the best ratio of stride length to frequency will be the fastest athlete.

My top recommended drills for speed are:

Sled pushes. Great for reinforcing proper sprint angle, sled sprints allow you to add resistance to speed work.

A-skips. An A-skip is a form drill that develops limb

mechanics by teaching an athlete how to properly drive his or her knees and arms.

Reaction sprints. Reaction sprints are when the athlete sprints based on a trigger, such as the coach dropping a tennis ball or clapping his hands. This develops fast reaction time, which is essential for athletes.

AGILITY

Agility is the ability to change direction quickly. It is broken down into two components known as pre-determined and reactionary. Pre-determined agility is what most people are training during agility drills where they know exactly which way they are going to go and the actions are planned. Reactionary agility is more like a game situation, where you're juking and moving around an opponent, and your body is moving based on your reactions in the game. Reactionary drills are randomized and are more relevant to the athletic population because they have a better carry-over from training to actual competition.

In order to increase overall agility, you must work on both the pre-determined and reactionary components. To develop pre-determined agility, I recommend agility ladders, cone drills, and mini-hurdles. These activities primarily improve coordination. To develop reactionary agility, which is true agility, I recommend randomizing your agility drills.

Agility training is needed for all sports, and there are certain sports which by their very nature actually develop agility. These include basketball, football, and soccer, all of which require frequent, rapid changes in direction.

Agility training improves the athlete's ability to change direction, increases the speed of direction changes, and improves body control when changing direction. Agility training also helps guard against injury by equipping the body to better avoid obstacles and manage external forces. However, in order to be effective, agility training must be sport-specific. Training drills must mimic what the athlete does on the court or on the field, otherwise the body enters the field of competition with muscle memories built around the wrong task.

My top recommended drills for agility are:

Five-ten-five drill. This one is also known as pro-agility and is the agility test done at the NFL Combine and the NBA Combine. The drill measures how quickly the athlete can travel five yards, stop on a dime, sprint another ten, change direction again, and sprint back five.

Dot drill. This drill uses a mat with five dots on it. Each dot has a number. The coach will yell out a series of numbers and the athlete must jump to the dot for each of those numbers in sequence as fast as possible.

Cone alley. For the cone alley drill, a series of cones is set up and the athlete must sprint to each one then change direction and movement. The drill can call for sprinting to one, shuffling to the next, then sprinting again to another; or it might call for sprinting to one then back pedaling to the next. They key is that the athlete sprints to a cone and only then receives the cue on how to change direction and which exercise to perform to the next cone.

QUICKNESS

Quickness is similar to speed but comes in short bursts, like the first few steps when sprinting or changing direction. Quickness is essential, for example, for a runner coming out of the gate whose first two steps cover a critical distance between points A and B that are only five feet apart. Quickness comes into play over very short distances.

To train for quickness, you can do first-step speed drills. One of the best ways to test for quickness is to measure a five-yard sprint or a three-yard sprint and track how fast the athlete is moving in the first three steps. In the NFL, defensive line players often drill with a 40-yard dash, during which the coach measures the first ten yards as well as the final outcome. This is known as a ten-yard split. It is not uncommon to see a defensive lineman that runs a 40-yard dash in 4.9 seconds have the same ten-yard split as a wide receiver that runs the dash in 4.3 seconds, because for the defensive lineman those first seconds off the line are critical. He must be cat-quick off the line, and those guys train for quickness aggressively.

My top recommended drills for quickness are:

40-yard start. A 40-yard is a 40-yard dash in which you focus mainly on the start. It is essentially a five-yard sprint drill.

Line jump sprint. In this drill, the athlete begins in front of a line, then jumps backwards to the line, and finally as soon as their feet hit the line, they sprint.

Ball drop sprint. For ball drops, the athlete gets into position watching the coach, who holds a tennis ball. The instant the coach drops the ball, the athlete sprints to it and must catch the ball before it bounces twice. The ball is allowed to bounce once, and must be caught off that first pop.

CHAPTER FIVE
Applying Plyometric Training for Athletes

Plyometric training is a special form of "jump training" that manipulates the stretch/shortening cycle in the body. Most people think of plyometric training as simple jump training; however, true plyometric training faster and much more intense. Because many people confuse plyometric training with something else, it has gotten a bad rap in the past. A lot of people think it is not safe for athletes and not generally effective, and consequently that the stress placed on the joint may outweigh the benefits of it.

The benefit of plyometric training is that it increases overall power. This power boost can increase vertical jump, strength, and speed of movement. It can also amplify pro-prioception, or awareness of when the body is jumping. To be sure, there are also drawbacks to plyometric training. It does place stress on the body, and if the athlete is not physically ready for certain drills, there is risk of a knee or ankle injury. It is important to work with a coach who is able to assess the individual's readiness for the training and provide immediate, proper feedback on form during the exercise.

Plyometric training should be performed at the beginning of any strength training workout. Because plyo training is demanding on the body, it should be done while the athlete is fresh and fully prepared. Running a plyometric drill at the end of the workout when the individual is tired and the muscles are spent dramatically increases the risk of injury.

It is safe to introduce plyometric training in athletes as young as ten years old. A ten-year-old can be coached on how to move his or her body in space and can learn how to safely and effectively perform the jumps. With athletes at any age, it is important to work progressively with plyometric training, not dive right into it without any preparation. The very first thing the athlete should be taught is proper landing technique. The landing is extremely important, because that's where injuries occur, including ACL tears to the knee and ankle sprains and fractures. The next step is simple jump training. With this foundation, the individual can progress to true plyometric training.

*CALL 610-567-3433 TODAY FOR A FREE CONSULTATION/
TRAINING SESSION AND TAKE YOUR GAME TO THE NEXT LEVEL*

CHAPTER SIX
Core Training for Athletes

Core training is a term that covers a broad range of activities. When people talk about the core, they think about the abs. In actuality, the core is everything from below the collar bone to just below the groin, on both the front and back sides of the body. Core training includes overall body stability and strengthening of all the muscles in that entire core region.

A lot of people want six-pack abs and only value the core for the sake of appearance, but the body's core is the root of all movement and is essential for elite performance in every sport. For the athlete, core training develops overall control of the trunk and the body. There is, in fact, no correlation between having six-pack abs and performing at a higher level. The appearance of the six-pack is more a function of body fat. An individual can have six-pack abs yet still not have a stable or strong core.

As far as core development, the last thing an athlete should do is any type of crunch. That old-school style of ab training with crunches is really detrimental to an athlete because it places a lot of stress on the spine and puts the body in a position that is a set-up for injury. Another exercise to avoid is side bends. This movement puts the back in an unhealthy position where the spine is being stretched. That movement creates searing forces on the spine and can injure the back. Any position that flexes or extends the spine should be avoided.

Core training for an athlete should utilize resistance movements and should focus on three types of exercises: anti-rotational, anti-extension, and anti-lateral flexion exercises. In this case, "anti" means resistance to the movement, so anti-rotational implies resisting a rotation, anti-extension means resisting an extension of the spine, and anti-lateral flexion means resisting a lateral flexion of the spine. All this resistance is accomplished by engaging the core musculature.

Anti-Extension: Plank Variations
Anti-Rotation: Band or Cable Pallof Press
Anti-Lateral Flexion: KB or DB Suitcase Carry

CHAPTER SEVEN
Injury Prevention

Injuries are happening more often today than ever before because kids are participating in sports in record numbers and are competing in far more games than past years. In a weekend tournament, a team might play an intense sport upwards of three or four games a day. Many children are also playing organized sports all year round. Their bodies aren't ready for that intensity or duration of exercise stress, and generally the kids are not properly trained or conditioned for that.

Every parent and coach should make it a priority to teach kids injury-prevention techniques and make this part of warm-ups and cool-downs. Injury prevention should also be incorporated into strength training programs. The bottom

line is that training should revolve around injury prevention
for athletes of all ages, and especially for the youth.

Obviously, an injured athlete cannot compete, so any
type of practice, or competition, or sports performance
training should focus on keeping the athlete healthy and
able to compete. What most people fail to consider are the
potential long-term effects of an injury. After one injury,
the athlete's likelihood for re-injury skyrockets. This is
especially true with serious injuries like tears, sprains,
and dislocations. These injuries have very high rates
of recurrence.

Some easy yet effective injury prevention techniques
include:

- Agility drills on a single leg to strengthen the ligaments
  surrounding the ankle
- Band resistance to improve joint integrity
- Corrective exercises to decrease compensation
- Mobility techniques included in warm-up
- Proper landing and deceleration technique

*CALL 610-567-3433 TODAY FOR A FREE CONSULTATION/
TRAINING SESSION AND TAKE YOUR GAME TO THE NEXT LEVEL*

CHAPTER EIGHT
Sports Nutrition

Sports nutrition is concerned with properly fueling the body to enable the athlete to reach full athletic potential. What you put in your body will drive what you put out on the field. If you fuel your body poorly, you are going to perform poorly.

Athletes need a well-balanced diet that incorporates proteins, carbohydrates, and healthy fats. Ideally an athlete's diet should be about 45 percent carbohydrates, 20 to 25 percent protein, and 30 to 35 percent fat. These nutrients should come from real meats, fruits, vegetables, and grains, not processed foods from boxes or cans. I counsel the athletes I train to shop around the edges of the supermarket where the fresh produce and meats are displayed, and to avoid the center aisles, which are filled with processed food.

Supplements are also important. Most athletes need to supplement protein in order to reach their protein goal. In general, an athlete should consume between 0.9 and 1.2 grams of protein for every pound of body weight each day. Protein is essential for healing and building muscle tissue. Athletes train frequently and in the process, they tear down muscle tissue. Adequate protein intake is essential to speed up this healing process. Supplementing with a protein shake (post-workout) will help muscles grow safely and effectively and in turn will help the athlete reach his or her performance goals.

CHAPTER NINE
Strength Training Myths

Over the years, a tremendous amount of strength training myths have circulated. It is surely one of the most misunderstood aspects of athletic fitness. Below are just a few of the myths I've heard through the years, along with the actual facts of the matter.

Myth: Weight training is not safe for young people.

Truth: Weight training is SAFE for young athletes. Bad coaches, on the other hand, are not. A well-educated and certified coach can create a balanced, safe, and effective training program for athletes at all levels and training ages.

Myth: Weight training will make you big and bulky

Truth: Properly designed athletic performance programs create a well-balanced athlete, not a meathead. If size is your main goal, a good coach will be able to create a program to build size and still maintain mobility. It is much more difficult for women to "bulk up" than for men. That's not to say it can't be done, but if you're concerned about maintaining a feminine form, weight training is not going to spoil that for you.

Myth: More is better.

Truth: Increased volume for athletes is not the answer. Athletes already put their body and central nervous system through enough with practices and games. If you are strength training at high volumes on top of that, you will over-train. The central nervous system is a sensitive beast, and a fatigued nervous system sets you up for injury.

Myth: I can find a professional anywhere.

Truth: Earlier, I said good coaches can create good programs. That's true; however, it may not be easy to find a good coach. Hundreds of fitness and personal training certifications are popping up every year, and anyone with a high school degree can become a Cross-Fit instructor or personal trainer. I recommend you find a coach with an undergraduate degree in exercise science or kinesiology and a certification from an accredited institute such as the National Strength and Conditioning Association (NSCA) or the National Academy of Sports Medicine (NASM). These coaches have been thoroughly educated on program design for clients of all skill levels and movement capabilities. I suggest you interview the coach before making a final decision. Ask them about their client history, training background, and education. After all, you are hiring this person to perform an important service to you.

Myth: Athletes should run for distance.

Truth: Unless your sport is distance running, there is small carryover in the athletic setting. Mind you, building an aerobic base is important, but there are other ways to accomplish that with much less wear and tear on the body.

Myth: Machines are safe.

Truth: Machines are not really all that safe. Your body is meant to move freely. Not everyone is built the same, therefore not everyone should be training at the same joint angles. Machines force every individual into a one-size-fits-all structure, and they limit motion, disallowing your body to move the way it is intended to move.

Myth: Weight training stunts your growth.

Truth: There is no scientific evidence for this notion. A stereotype exists of the short, stocky weightlifter that has given rise to this idea, but if anything, science supports the idea that strength training increases stress, the good kind of stress, on bones, making them stronger and more resilient. Again, there is no evidence that this has ever happened to anyone.

Myth: Anyone can create an effective weight-training program.

Truth: As I mentioned earlier, exercise science is, well, a science. It encompasses a rich body of knowledge, and many people study for years to pursue this profession. Only those who are certified and educated to do so should design a weight-training program intended for athletes, of for anyone, for that matter.

CHAPTER TEN
How to Create the Best Training Program

The best training program develops all facets of athletic performance. It will emphasize injury prevention, and then focus on strength, power, speed, agility flexibility, mobility, and body composition. Progress will be measured frequently, and programs will be progressive in nature.

When parents look to put their child in a training program, there are definitely some things they need to consider.

It is crucial to confirm that it is something that the child wants to do. If the child isn't interested or isn't dedicated to improving his athletic capabilities, he may not give a hundred percent when training. It's also possible the child could be injured if he is not focused or if he isn't giving it all when training.

Find a good facility and an even better coach. You need a well-educated coach that has a good track record of successful clients. You should also insist on a coach who focuses on injury prevention. The candidate coach should put your athlete through some sort of movement screening before agreeing to train him or her. Immediately discard any coach that doesn't conduct a consultation or evaluation; without the information from such an evaluation, the coach can't possibly create a sound program for the athlete. Finally, look for someone who has a degree in exercise science or kinesiology and a couple of certifications from accredited institutes such as NSCA or NASM.

Another element of a quality training program is that it must cover both in-season and off-season training. The need for off-season training is fairly clear, but many parents/coaches don't realize the importance of training during the competitive season. Strength must be maintained throughout a season, after all you don't need to peak in the beginning of the season. A decreased training volume/frequency should be prescribed, but intensity should remain high.

With its freedom from the schedule and fatigue of competition, the off-season offers time to really drive gains. These might be gains in weight, strength, speed, accuracy, or whatever the sport requires. The off-season is also a good time to rehab any lingering injuries and to address performance deficits that surfaced during the past season and get them cleaned up prior to the next round of competition.

A good off-season training program will be broken down into three phases, with each phase focusing on a different overall goal and each phase progressing. Most off-season training programs will last about three months, with each month having a different focus.

Phase 1 is the time to work on stabilization. This means getting the athlete used to moving himself under resistance and ensuring the form is good.

Phase 2 would then emphasize building strength. This means increasing weight-bearing exercises and working upward to increasingly heavy loads.

Phase 3 is a high-intensity phase leading immediately into the season. The objective is for the athlete to perform strength movements powerful fashion to closely mimic sport.

While each phase has a focus, the phases build on each other. In the third month, the elements from the two prior months are not forgotten, otherwise the athlete would lose all of his size and strength gains by the end of the power phase.

In-season training is vitally important because if you don't train, you quickly lose everything you worked for in the off-season. The goal of in-season training is to maintain the benefits and advancements captured during off-season training. If you are an athlete who doesn't get much playing time during the season, you must treat the competitive season like an off-season and train hard.

To guide your in-season and off-season development, this book includes actual sample training programs for middle school and high school athletes in a couple of different sports. These examples can be modified based on the specific developmental requirements of your athlete's sport and age and capability level.

PROGRAM
Off-Season High School Field Hockey
or Soccer Player

NAME: **PHASE : 1**
SPORT: FIELD HOCKEY
DAY 1

FOAM ROLL: All major muscle groups for 30 sec

ACTIVATION/CORRECTIVES

DYNAMIC: High knees, butt kicks, knee hug, pull back,
10 walking lunges, 10 squats, 10 lateral lunge, 10 yards
Frankenstein walks, A-skips, B-Skips, power skips
for height, power skips for distance

ACTIVATION: 5/5 Single-leg glute bridges, 10 scapular push-ups,
10 band pull-aparts

AGILITY LADDER
BOX JUMPS: 5x3
MEDICINE BALL OVERHEAD LAUNCH 5X3

A1) KETTLEBELL SWING

Date	Sets	Reps	Notes	Set 1	Set 2	Set 3	Set 4	Set 5	Set 6
	3	10	Flex glutes						
	3	10	At top						
	4	8	Drive hips						
	3	8	Through						

A2) BAND TERMINAL KNEE EXTENSION

Date	Sets	Reps	Notes	Set 1	Set 2	Set 3	Set 4	Set 5	Set 6
	3	10e	Lock knee						
	3	15e	Fully						
	4	15e							
	3	10e							

B1) KETTLEBELL GOBLET SQUAT

Date	Sets	Reps	Notes	Set 1	Set 2	Set 3	Set 4	Set 5	Set 6
	3	10							
	3	8							
	4	8							
	3	6	Deload						

B2) ANKLE WALL MOBILIZATION

Date	Sets	Reps	Notes	Set 1	Set 2	Set 3	Set 4	Set 5	Set 6
	3	8/8							
	3	8/8							
	4	8/8							
	3	8/8							

B3) PLANK

Date	Sets	Reps	Notes	Set 1	Set 2	Set 3	Set 4	Set 5	Set 6
	3	30s							
	3	45s							
	4	60s							
	3	60s							

C1) KETTLEBELL DEADLIFT

Date	Sets	Reps	Notes	Set 1	Set 2	Set 3	Set 4	Set 5	Set 6
	3	8							
	3	8							
	4	6							
	3	8							

C2) GLUTE BRIDGE (PLATE OR KETTLEBELL)

Date	Sets	Reps	Notes	Set 1	Set 2	Set 3	Set 4	Set 5	Set 6
	3	10	Pause/Contract						
	3	8	For 2 seconds						
	4	8	At the top						
	3	6	Drive hips						

C3) BIRD DOG

Date	Sets	Reps	Notes	Set 1	Set 2	Set 3	Set 4	Set 5	Set 6
	3	6e							
	3	8e							
	4	8e							
	3	8e							

C2) SPRINTS

Date	Sets	Reps	Notes	Set 1	Set 2	Set 3	Set 4	Set 5	Set 6
	4	3	10 yards						
	4	4	10 yards						
	5	4	10 yards						
	4	3	10 yards						

C3) SLED PULL/PUSH

Date	Sets	Reps	Notes	Set 1	Set 2	Set 3	Set 4	Set 5	Set 6
	3	20yd							
	3	30yd							
	4	30yd							

NA E **HASE**

S RT IE H E

A

FOAM ROLL: All major muscle groups for 30 sec

ACTIVATION/CORRECTIVES

DYNAMIC: High knees, butt kicks, knee hug, pull back, 10 walking lunge, 10 squats, 10 lateral lunges, 10 yards Frankenstein walks, A-skips, B-Skips, power skips for height, power skips for distance

ACTIVATION: T-spine mobilization, Bear crawl

AGILITY DOTS
LATERAL HURDLE JUMP 4X4 EACH WAY
ROTATIONAL MB THROW 4X4 EACH WAY

A1) DUMBBELL PUSH JERK

Date	Sets	Reps	Notes	Set 1	Set 2	Set 3	Set 4	Set 5	Set 6
	3	5e							
	3	5e							
	4	4e							
	3	3e	Deload						

A2) BAND PULL-APARTS

Date	Sets	Reps	Notes	Set 1	Set 2	Set 3	Set 4	Set 5	Set 6
	3	10							
	3	10							
	4	10							
	3	6							

B1) PUSH-UP

Date	Sets	Reps	Notes	Set 1	Set 2	Set 3	Set 4	Set 5	Set 6
	3	6	Use blocks						
	3	6							
	4	8							
	3	4	No blocks						

B2) KETTLEBELL CHOP

Date	Sets	Reps	Notes	Set 1	Set 2	Set 3	Set 4	Set 5	Set 6
	3	6e	Straight arms						
	3	8e							
	4	8e							
	3	6e							

B3) BAND LO-HI ROW

Date	Sets	Reps	Notes	Set 1	Set 2	Set 3	Set 4	Set 5	Set 6
	3	10e	1/2/1						
	3	8e							
	4	8e	Step back						
	3	8e							

C1) BAND-ASSISTED PULL-UP

Date	Sets	Reps	Notes	Set 1	Set 2	Set 3	Set 4	Set 5	Set 6
	3	6							
	3	8							
	4	8							
	3	5							

C2) FLUTTER KICKS

Date	Sets	Reps	Notes	Set 1	Set 2	Set 3	Set 4	Set 5	Set 6
	3	50							
	3	50							
	4	50							
	3	50							

C3) MEDICINE BALL SLAM

Date	Sets	Reps	Notes	Set 1	Set 2	Set 3	Set 4	Set 5	Set 6
	3	10							
	3	10							
	4	10							
	3	10							

D1) ROPE SLAMS

Date	Sets	Reps	Notes	Set 1	Set 2	Set 3	Set 4	Set 5	Set 6
	1	100							
	1	100							
	1	100							
	3	40							

D2) BUILDING LAPS

Date	Sets	Reps	Notes	Set 1	Set 2	Set 3	Set 4	Set 5	Set 6
	2		Use watch						
	3								
	4								
	5								

NA E   HASE
S RT   IE H E
A

FOAM ROLL: All major muscle groups for 30 sec

ACTIVATION/CORRECTIVES

DYNAMIC: High knees, butt kicks, knee hug, pull back, 10 walking lunge, 10 Squat , 10 Lateral Lunge, 10 yards Frankenstein walks, A-skips, B-Skips, power skips for height, power skips for distance

ACTIVATION: 5/5 Single leg glute bridges, 10 scapular push-ups, 10 band pull-aparts

CONE ALLEY
MULTI-DIRECTIONAL HURDLE JUMPS

A1) 2 HAND KETTLEBELL GOBLET CLEAN

Date	Sets	Reps	Notes	Set 1	Set 2	Set 3	Set 4	Set 5	Set 6
	3	5							
	3	6	Increase wt						
	4	6	Increase wt						
	3	4	Deload						

A2) WALL ANKLE MOBILIZATION

Date	Sets	Reps	Notes	Set 1	Set 2	Set 3	Set 4	Set 5	Set 6
	3	10e							
	3	10e							
	3	10e							
	3	10e							

B1) KETTLEBELL ROMANIAN DEADLIFT

Date	Sets	Reps	Notes	Set 1	Set 2	Set 3	Set 4	Set 5	Set 6
	3	8							
	4	8							
	4	6							
	3	6							

B2) DUMBBELL FLOOR PRESS

Date	Sets	Reps	Notes	Set 1	Set 2	Set 3	Set 4	Set 5	Set 6
	3	10							
	3	8							
	4	8							
	3	6	Deload						

B3) TRX FALLOUT

Date	Sets	Reps	Notes	Set 1	Set 2	Set 3	Set 4	Set 5	Set 6
	3	6							
	3	8							
	4	10							
	3	10							

C1) DUMBBELL/KETTLEBELL WALKING LUNGES

Date	Sets	Reps	Notes	Set 1	Set 2	Set 3	Set 4	Set 5	Set 6
	3	10e							
	4	8e							
	4	8e							
	3	8e	Deload						

C2) RECLINE ROW

Date	Sets	Reps	Notes	Set 1	Set 2	Set 3	Set 4	Set 5	Set 6
	3	10	1 sec pause						
	4	10							
	4	8	Move feet further away						
	3	10							

C3) T-SPINE BENCH MOBILIZATION

Date	Sets	Reps	Notes	Set 1	Set 2	Set 3	Set 4	Set 5	Set 6
	3	8							
	4	8							
	4	8							
	3	8							

D1) SPRINTS

Date	Sets	Reps	Notes	Set 1	Set 2	Set 3	Set 4	Set 5	Set 6
	4	20yd							
	5	20yd							
	6	20yd							
	8	20yd							

R GRA
In-Season Middle School Athlete

NA E   **HASE**

S RT   IE H E

A

FOAM ROLL: All major muscle groups for 30 sec

ACTIVATION/CORRECTIVES

DYNAMIC: High knees, butt kicks, knee hug, pull back, 10 walking lunges, 10 squats, 10 lateral lunges, 10 yards Frankenstein walks, A-skips, B-Skips, power skips for height, power skips for distance

A1) PUSH-UP

Date	Sets	Reps	Notes	Set 1	Set 2	Set 3	Set 4	Set 5	Set 6
	3	10							
	3	10							
	3	12							
	2	8							

A2) TRX RECLINE ROW

Date	Sets	Reps	Notes	Set 1	Set 2	Set 3	Set 4	Set 5	Set 6
	3	10							
	3	12							
	3	15							
	2	10							

B1) BODYWEIGHT SPLIT SQUAT

Date	Sets	Reps	Tempo	Set 1	Set 2	Set 3	Set 4	Set 5	Set 6
	3	8/8e	3/1/1						
	3	8/8e	3/1/1						
	3	6/6e	3/1/1						
	2	6/6e							

B2) BEAR CRAWL

Date	Sets	Reps	Distance	Set 1	Set 2	Set 3	Set 4	Set 5	Set 6
	3		12 yd						
	3		15 yd						
	4		20 yd						
	3		12 yd						

C1) BAND PULL-APARTS

Date	Sets	Reps	Notes	Set 1	Set 2	Set 3	Set 4	Set 5	Set 6
	3	10	1 sec pause						
	3	10							
	3	12							
	2	10							

C2) PLANK

Date	Sets	Reps	Notes	Set 1	Set 2	Set 3	Set 4	Set 5	Set 6
	3	35s							
	3	45s							
	4	55s							
	3	55s							

D1) ROPES

Date	Sets	Reps	Notes	Set 1	Set 2	Set 3	Set 4	Set 5	Set 6
	4	40							
	4	40							
	5	40							
	4	40							

D2) MB SLAMS

Date	Sets	Reps	Notes	Set 1	Set 2	Set 3	Set 4	Set 5	Set 6
	3	10							
	3	12							
	4	15							
	3	10							

NA E   HASE
S RT   IE H E
A

FOAM ROLL: All major muscle groups for 30 sec

ACTIVATION/CORRECTIVES

DYNAMIC: High knees, butt kicks, knee hug, pull back, 10 walking lunges, 10 squats, 10 lateral lunges, 10 yards Frankenstein walks, A-skips, B-Skips, power skips for height, power skips for distance

A1) CADENCED BODYWEIGHT SQUAT

Date	Sets	Reps	Tempo	Set 1	Set 2	Set 3	Set 4	Set 5	Set 6
	3	10	2/1/2						
	3	10							
	3	8							
	2	8							

A2) SQUAT JUMPS

Date	Sets	Reps	Notes	Set 1	Set 2	Set 3	Set 4	Set 5	Set 6
	3	5							
	3	5	w/MB						
	3	5	w/MB						
	2	5							

B1) HALF-KNEELING SINGLE-ARM DUMBBELL PRESS

Date	Sets	Reps	Notes	Set 1	Set 2	Set 3	Set 4	Set 5	Set 6
	3	10/10							
	3	8/8							
	3	6/6							
	3	6	Deload						

B2) BAND-ASSISTED PULL-UP

Date	Sets	Reps	Notes	Set 1	Set 2	Set 3	Set 4	Set 5	Set 6
	3	8							
	3	8							
	3	10							
	2	6							

C1) BAND PULL-THROUGH

Date	Sets	Reps	Notes	Set 1	Set 2	Set 3	Set 4	Set 5	Set 6
	3	10							
	3	10							
	3	8							
	2	8							

C2) BAND BELLY PRESS

Date	Sets	Reps	Notes	Set 1	Set 2	Set 3	Set 4	Set 5	Set 6
	3	10/10							
	3	12/12							
	3	12/12							
	3	10/10							

D1) SLED ROW

Date	Sets	Reps	Distance	Set 1	Set 2	Set 3	Set 4	Set 5	Set 6
	4		20yd						
	4		20yd						
	5		20yd						
	2		20yd						

Made in the USA
Middletown, DE
11 February 2015